Train Your Dog in One Hour

Train Your Dog in One Hour

Sandy Butler

Glenbridge Publishing Ltd.

Book Illustrations
Patricia Hobbs

Library of Congress Catalog Number: LC 98-72111

International Standard Book Number: 0-944435-45-9

10   9   8   7

To the wonderful dogs in my life:

Bull

Ginger

Jake

Libby

Reno

Z

and my first and most special dog,

Eric

Contents

Introduction   1

Chapter 1   What Dog is Best For You 11

Chapter 2   Training Your Dog 69

Chapter 3   General Care of Your Dog 131

Chapter 4   First Aid for Your Pet 159

Chapter 5   Questions and Answers 183

Bibliography 203

Index 205

INTRODUCTION

I've always been interested in dogs. I was born with that interest, and I started training dogs before I knew I was doing it. My parents got me a dog when I was four years old, and that dog became my best friend. As a child, I was on the chubby side, so sometimes my schoolmates made fun of me making me feel terrible. When I got home from school, my parents were usually gone—dad was working and mom was off at a meeting of one of her many organizations. There I was, left with my dog and my nanny, crying and miserable. So I cried to my dog and became very close to Eric, my Irish Setter. Happily, he lived a long time, until I was sixteen years old, when he died of a heart

attack. Of course, I was deeply saddened by his loss, and I slept with his collar under my pillow for the next two years.

Our pets provide companionship, comfort, security, entertainment, and unconditional love. When your pet dies, it is completely understandable that you are grieving. People often mask their grief because society does not easily support the right to grieve for an animal. Many feel isolated and embarrassed and even have trouble eating, sleeping, or going to work for months after a pet's death. A friend who has a pet is likely to provide understanding and offer help to get through the mourning. There are support groups for those who lose pets, and you can get individual or group counseling as well.

Being so close to my dog taught me how to train using positive reinforcement. I didn't understand the method I had come to use, a method that seemed more instinctual to me, but it became a method I used to train every other dog that came into my possession. My dogs always did everything I wanted, even though I didn't know I was actually training them. I even trained a horse named "Killer." No one else

could get on him except me—not even real cowboys. He used to rear and knock everybody off. I got on him and from the first day we were best of friends, and he did everything I wanted.

The essence of my training is to get into the mind of the animal. If you understand that your dog wants to please you, you will work with your dog in a positive way, and when you do this, your success is assured.

Sometime ago I had a business in a small mountain community in Colorado. Right next door was a dog shelter. There was hardly ever anyone at the shelter because the person in charge was always out taking care of problems. Almost every day, people would stop at my store accompanied by their dog. They would ask me to take care of Rover until someone became available at the dog shelter. I would beg these people to take their dogs back home with the promise that I would show up at their front door and train their dog. I told them, "If I can train your dog in an hour or less to follow commands, will you keep it?" Training was so easy for me I couldn't understand why others appeared to have so much trouble. Within an

hour of when I walked in the door, their dog was completely trained. The dogs were coming to their owners when called, sitting, lying down, staying—doing everything their owners wanted their dogs to do.

Word got out—big time. Before I knew it I was being called all the time by everybody who wanted his or her dog trained. I was out training dogs until 11 or 12 o'clock at night! I needed help—real bad. So I created a video, demonstrating my training method. I figured that if it's easy for me to do, then others could learn these simple techniques also. That one was so well-received, I made a second video. Together, they offer everything you need to know to have a well-trained dog and thus a very happy owner.

Dogs want to mind you more than anything else in the world. They just don't understand what you're saying. I can show you how to break through that language barrier through positive communication using simple hand and voice commands. Bad habits will be broken, and your dog will do about anything you wish.

For some time I've been appearing on radio

and television across the U.S, Canada, and England. It's just a wonderful feeling to share ideas that help dog owners. With letters coming in regularly from all over the country with happy stories about our training methods, we wanted to share our training methods with you.

1

WHAT DOG
IS BEST FOR YOU

Where to Get a Dog

Let's assume you don't have a dog but you want one. Your question is one all prospective dog owners ask. What kind of dog should I get? That's an important question. First of all, I'm a firm believer in getting a dog from a shelter. We all like to think that all those lovely dogs in shelters across the country will find a marvelous, loving home, but unfortunately, that is not the case. When you obtain your dog from a shelter, the odds are very good that you are saving that dog's life. There are usually all kinds of purebreds available at shelters as well as many lovable mixed breeds. Don't sell those mixed

breed dogs short. They can make excellent companions and pets. And they may not be predisposed to certain ailments that afflict expensive, purebred animals.

There are 3500 hard-working animal shelters in the United States. Approximately 12 million animals are abandoned to shelters each year, and about 8 million are euthanized there. One female dog and her offspring can produce 67,000 dogs in six years. Every day in the U.S. 70,000 puppies and kittens are born. For every person born, seven puppies and kittens are born. The odds of an animal surviving a shelter and being adopted into a loving home is 1 in 4. Go to your pet shelter if you want a pet. You will be doing an animal a great service, finding him a loving home. You may join the millions of people who love their pets like no other.

A national survey cited that 88 percent of Americans would lay down their lives for their pet. Sixty-six percent of Americans insist that their pet is an actual child. Forty-four percent say their pet always sleeps in bed with them. Twenty-two percent feel closer to their pet than their spouse.

Children and Dogs

I think it's wonderful for children to have a dog. But you don't want to go out and get just any kind of dog because Mr. any-kind-of-dog may not be right for your child. So many people see that cute puppy and can't resist. But a good choice takes some careful thought and no little planning. Some dogs will put up with children pulling their tails and poking their eyes. But there are other dogs that just won't tolerate such behavior. Check the section later in this chapter and also the many books in your library on dog breeds to help you determine what type of dog might be best.

When you go to a shelter to get your dog, you will find many varieties of dogs waiting just for you. They are just heartbroken and may have been brought in by an owner who had to leave town or had gone through a divorce. These dogs all want new homes. If you have to return a dog to the shelter for behavior problems, that means you're not communicating with your animal, and you need to read this book, maybe more than once.

You don't always have to get a puppy. Young dogs are not always best for children, or for adults either. Often starting out with a dog two to four years old can make life easier for you and your family. Your own lifestyle will help you determine what is best for you.

Some breeds that are recognized as being very good with children are Golden Retrievers or Golden Retriever mixes. I've had wonderful experiences with Greyhounds also, and they're great with children. Labs and Lab mixes are also wonderful with children. That Irish Setter I grew up with was a fine dog, and I would recommend the breed for any family. These breeds and many others can be perfect for children.

Golden Retrievers seem to stay young longer than most dogs. They can go through puppyhood for two to three years. But they are also easily trainable using my method. If you get a Golden Retriever mix, usually the shelter can tell you what he's mixed with. Then go to the library and read up on the other breed, and that will give you a general idea of the personality of the dog.

I was over at a client's house recently and was told she had just gotten rid of a Greyhound

that she said was growling at her child. When we talked about it, I discovered that the dog was not growling but smiling! Many dogs smile, and the Greyhound often takes the prize. The baby sitter had thought the dog was angry when it "bared its teeth." Please, don't get rid of your nice Greyhound just because he has a sense of humor.

Greyhounds are wonderful dogs that get along not only with children but with the elderly at nursing homes. We generally believe that all a Greyhound wants to do is run, but even when they are trained for racing, they only race for maybe thirty seconds every three days. That's not a long time. The rest of the time they sit in cages, usually bored and unhappy. If you let them up on your sofa, they will remain there forever. They can't give children, and the rest of us, enough love.

An Irish Setter is a great dog for children. Mine was the nicest dog you've ever seen. He was wonderful with me and with my friends. Sometimes this breed likes to roam, so you will have to be sure to have a good fence and a place for him to stay. If you let this, or any other type

DOGS LOVE TO FOLLOW
THEIR MASTERS TO SCHOOL.

of dog, roam, he could get stolen, or get into a horrible dogfight, and you could lose him.

When a Dog is Dangerous

Almost four million people in the United States were bitten by a dog last year. Children between the ages of five and nine have the greatest risk. Many don't know how to act around dogs and must be taught what to do and what not to do. Of course you always need to watch your children when they are around dogs that you don't know. If you're going to visit a home with an unknown dog, explain to your children that they should never run right over to a strange dog and put their faces near the dog's face. A dog often thinks that eye contact is an act of aggression. If your child is too young to understand that, he or she must be watched very carefully.

Often when a dog sees children playing hard or fighting, the dog may become nervous and may be prone to bite. If you understand the dog's reaction, you will be better able to make friends with a strange dog and to protect your children at the same time. If, for any reason, a

dog knocks you to the ground, you should roll into a ball and remain still. Do not scream. Cover your ears and head with your arms and hands. Teach your children to do the same.

If a child is afraid of a dog, instruct the child to remain perfectly still and not to run. If the dog decides he wants to bite, running from him makes the biting even more likely. Ordinarily, dogs are not dangerous and are remarkably friendly animals. But there are exceptions, and both adults and children should be prepared if confronted by an unfriendly dog.

Many dog owners train their dogs to attack strangers who approach their houses. Dogs are often put to sleep because of what the owners have taught them. But the dog's behavior is not the dog's fault. Perhaps the owners of these animals should be locked up!

I believe that all children should have a dog, however, a dog they will quickly grow to love and a dog who will repay that love many times over.

Dogs and Babies

I received a call from my niece in California

a couple of months ago. She was expecting a baby. She had been told to start paying less attention to her dogs because the baby was coming and she wasn't going to be able to give her dogs as much attention as she usually did. She remembered that I knew something about dogs, so she asked me whether that advice was right. I had to disagree with her well-meaning friend. I told her that there were lots of things she could do when the new baby arrived to make everybody feel loved and at home. As soon as she walked in with the baby and had placed the baby in the crib, I told her to walk over to her dog, put her arm around her dog and say to the dog, "Fido, Mine, Fido, Mine." Point to your dog and point to yourself. Then walk over to your baby, pick her up, give her a big hug and tell Fido, "Baby, Mine, Baby, Mine." Make a big deal out of it. Then point to your dog and say, "Baby, Fido's, Baby, Fido's." It may sound silly, but believe me it works. Your dog will come to understand that he is loved just as the new baby is loved. And your dog will quickly learn to love the new baby. In this way Fido will learn to tolerate less attention than he received before.

That Mixed Breed Dog

Everyone loves a mutt—not my favorite expression. We all smile and get fuzzy warm feelings when we hear stories about the heroic exploits of a smart mixed breed dog reported regularly on television or in stories from the movies. Such a dog is often created from unknown connections, with the face of one breed, the tail of another, and perhaps the body of a third breed. They are sweet, charming, and often we can't resist them—particularly when they are puppies. We hear on the nightly news of dogs who survive unbelievable odds and need a new home. Hundreds of calls come in to the television station, all wanting to save the dog and to give him a home. Yet the decision to adopt a dog should not be made emotionally. Much thought and preparation are required.

I happen to like mixed breed dogs. I think they're absolutely wonderful. They have fewer health problems and are lots of fun. And mixed breeds are by far the most prevalent dog. There are many more "Brownies" than Cocker Spaniels. There are also tens of thousands of "Blackies"

and don't overlook "Spot." Many people ignore these fine dogs just because they think they want a purebred. Consider a mixed breed dog seriously when you go to the shelter. You may want to bring one home. They're really wonderful dogs.

As I have said, for many a puppy may not be the best choice for a pet. They have enormous energy, and you must train them not to chew and to go potty at the appropriate time and place. Older dogs may be too tired to chew your furniture and are easier to potty train. That older dog could be the perfect answer to your needs, and you will be able to avoid some of the special problems dog owners must face when adopting a new puppy. Of course older dogs may have special problems of their own. Sometimes older dogs have been abused or neglected by their former owners and may cower when you lift your hand to give a command. Sometimes they can be aggressive if they feel threatened. It might require more patience to get the dog used to a normal environment, but the training can be done in an hour or less with positive communication. You as his new master must remain

calm and assured. If you show worry and anxiety, he will too. Dogs are wonderfully social, active creatures and should lose their bad habits with love and careful training.

What Kind Of Dog For You?

Before making a selection you must look at yourself and your family. Are you a person who wants a shorthaired dog? Are you a clean freak? If you're not, you won't want a Great Pyrenees that will shed and drool all over your house. There are many shorthaired dogs that also shed, so if you need more information than you will find in this book, you'll need to go to your local library and read about different breeds of dogs. Perhaps you want a dog for your family, for the children. Perhaps you are a hunter and think it would be great to have a dog to retrieve that bird you've been trying to shoot for the last thirty-five years. If you live in the suburbs, perhaps you've always wanted to be a shepherd. Those sheep you are about to purchase require the services of a herd dog. All these problems need to be resolved before you run out and purchase that cute puppy with those sad loving eyes.

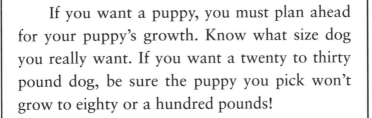

If you want a puppy, you must plan ahead for your puppy's growth. Know what size dog you really want. If you want a twenty to thirty pound dog, be sure the puppy you pick won't grow to eighty or a hundred pounds!

A Shelter or a Breeder

Did you know that one million people own a black or yellow Labrador Retriever? It's the nation's most popular purebred dog. If you have your heart set on a purebred dog, a dog shelter is still a great place to get your pet. If you want to go to a breeder, not just any breeder will do. You must be very selective since some breeders are not as reputable as others. They may do too much inbreeding, causing serious problems for the dogs as well as their eventual owners. Excessive inbreeding causes health problems, possible breathing problems, and often hip problems, all of which could shorten an animal's life and could generate large veterinarian bills. Call the breeder's references, and check out the puppies as well as their parents. Call former customers and find out about the health of their dogs and

whether the dog owners have any complaints about the breeding.

Are Two Dogs Better Than One?

Look who's talking! I've got six dogs! Well, not everyone should have six dogs, but I can easily make a case for having two dogs. Sometimes having two dogs is easier than just one. They keep each other company. They can run and play with each other, even though they sometimes want double attention. You then have to teach them that you need your time and space also and are not on call for your dogs every minute of the day. But dogs rarely get bored when they have a pal to be with and play with. They can end up loving each other so much that they grieve like humans if one dies. Dogs need friends just like people, so think about two dogs instead of just one.

Then there was Toby, a mixed breed Dachshund and Beagle. He was just full of life. He destroyed everything in sight, from mattresses to pillows, glasses, handbags—anything at all. His master sent him to obedience school. That calmed him a little bit, but soon he was back to his old

destructive ways. One day his master performed what seemed at the time to be a courageous act. He went out and obtained a buddy, a big fat Basset Hound called Amos. From the day Amos walked into the house, Toby became a different dog. Now he had a buddy! Toby protected Amos, who was not in the best of health. His master built a ramp for Amos so he wouldn't have to climb the stairs to get into the house. Amos still had trouble navigating the ramp, so Toby got behind his pal and pushed him up the ramp. A twenty pound dog was pushing a sixty-five pound dog. Toby never chewed another household item again.

Preparing Your Home for Your New Dog

Before you get your dog, be sure your home is ready for an animal. Do you have a fence in your yard? If you're not able to put up a fence, you have to ask yourself whether you should own a dog. If you live in an apartment, you have to be sure you can take your dog out without lots of problems.

Make sure you have a place for your dog, a place for him to lie down. If you don't mind

your dog lying anywhere in your house, then your problem is simplified. If you bring a puppy into your house, you must be in a position to watch him attentively until he's potty trained. While this procedure ordinarily takes no more than twenty-four hours, it is vitally important that this be accomplished efficiently and thoroughly. If you plan to confine your dog to a kennel for eight to ten hours a day because you have to go to work, think again about owning a dog. Tying your dog with a leash all day is even worse, but we all have seen way too many cases when dogs are mistreated in this way.

Make sure to keep things out of the way of your dog that could hurt him. Medicine should not be kept in low cabinets. Your dog can't read labels. Fido would be happy to eat whatever he finds in those cabinets, and such an excursion could cost him his life.

Many people like to keep their dogs in the garage in cold weather. But be sure that antifreeze is out of the way and carefully sealed. Antifreeze ingested by your dog can be fatal in a very short time. While there are some brands that are less harmful to pets, it's better to keep

such products totally out of reach of animals—and children also.

New puppies like to chew on all kinds of things, but if they show a taste for electric wires, both you and your puppy can be in trouble. The shock from a live wire can kill a puppy. Special "wraps" are available to make them harder to chew, but it would be better to have all wires out of reach of puppies.

Be sure you have the finances to be able to take your dog to a veterinarian. You should plan to take your dog to a vet at least twice a year to get him checked and to get his shots. Your pet should also be spayed or neutered. If you get your dog from a shelter, this procedure is part of the fee. There are enough dogs roaming the streets of our large cities to keep city officials working almost forever in an attempt to round them up. Responsible dog owners neuter or spay their dogs.

Spaying or neutering your dog will go far to cut the enormous over-population of dogs. Walk the halls of animal shelters as I have done and see those dozens of eyes just begging you to take them home with you. Then you will see the

importance of neutering your dog. And not only will you improve the odds of dogs leading reasonable and happy lives, but a neutered dog usually makes for a better behaved dog. They don't just sit around listless as many believe, but they still have lots of fun and retain their same personalities—minus some of the neurotic things they did before.

Slavery is Illegal

How many times do you drive by a house and see a dog tied to a chain, totally ignored by all. We are all attracted to that cute puppy with those winsome eyes. Yet, how many dog owners take their puppy home, pet him twice, and then tie him up in the backyard. Soon that cute puppy grows into Super Dog, and there he is— still tied up in the backyard, fed twice a day, but otherwise ignored. If this is your plan, please think again about purchasing a dog.

It's best to keep your dog indoors in the winter. They suffer the same ills of winter as we humans do—frostbite, dry and cracked paws, hypothermia, and much more. Dogs can freeze to death outdoors in the winter, and it happens

to many every year—even with a doghouse. If you must put your dog into a doghouse, do this only for a short time. If you feed your dogs outdoors, do not use a metal bowl. Your dog's tongue could freeze directly to the bowl.

Your Dog is Your Friend—Take Him With You

It is important that you bond with your puppy or new older dog. If you are a working person, get your dog on a weekend so you can be with your dog as much as possible before you have to go back to work on Monday. If you have to run to the grocery store or post office, take your dog with you. The more you can be with your dog, the faster you will bond. And the more you bond the better dog you're going to have and the easier he will be to train. Of course, you must be sensitive to the temperature in the car while Fido is patiently waiting for you to come out of the grocery store. If it's seventy degrees outside, it can get very hot in your car. Be sure you roll your windows down far enough for air to circulate but not far enough for the dog to jump out. In the wintertime, be careful that Fido doesn't get too cold. In other words,

think about the comfort of your dog as you would yourself.

Breed Differences

Humans have been breeding dogs for at least ten thousand years. During the last two hundred years, dogs have been bred for size, coat, and color. Often, dogs have been bred for temperament.

Northern breeds, such as the Husky, Elkhound, the Japanese Akita, and Chow Chow have powerful shoulders and dense coats. They have great stamina and with their dense coats, they shed a lot.

Guard dogs have a special personality. These animals, such as the Bernese, Great Pyrenees, Dobermans, and Boxers were bred for protection. If you have a special need for this breed of dog, you should investigate the many possibilities available.

Herding breeds, such as Collies and shepherd dogs, were bred to help shepherds and farmers. They are loyal and energetic but may bark when excited and sometimes have a tendency to nip.

Then there are those dogs built for speed. Greyhounds, Whippets, and Afghan Hounds fall into this category. They are loving animals and great pets.

Sporting dogs are often particularly affectionate. They were bred to respond to human commands. Setters, Pointers, Spaniels, and Retrievers are representative of this group.

There are scent hounds who have been bred to work in packs and follow the weakest trails. They include Bloodhounds, Basset Hounds, and Beagles.

How about those terriers? They were originally bred to chase small game and vermin. They are now energetic dogs, often can exercise themselves, but sometimes are powerful barkers.

There are sex differences also. The male dog's brain receives a surge of hormone just before birth. That's why male dogs tend to grow bigger and are generally more territorial and dominant. The female dog's brain is more neutral at birth. At puberty, female hormones can increase possessive behavior and can alter the dog's mood. Neutering just before sexual maturity usually can ensure that your dog's existing personality will continue.

WHEN A BEARDED COLLIE
IS NOT A
BEARDED COLLIE.

You may want to check the following partial list of dog breeds and some of their characteristics. Of course there are hundreds of breeds. If you want a complete list, check with your local library. Some breeds are extremely rare, and if you can find a good breeder, they may be very expensive.

Breeds of Dogs

Here is a short list of some of the more popular breeds and their characteristics.

Afghan Hound: Highly individual personality, sure-footed, agile, full of stamina. His coat requires regular care and grooming—aristocratic appearance—an elegant dog.

Akita: A native of Japan, good-natured, alert and docile—very affectionate with family and thrives on human companionship, but can be testy. They are considered a symbol of good health in Japan.

Basenji: The "barkless" dog—smart and proud, a fine silky coat. He is intelligent, courageous, endearing, and gentle as a kitten. He cleans

himself as does a cat—a perfect dog for an im-
maculate housekeeper.

Bearded Collie: Valued as a sheepdog, hard
workers, adept, strong and agile—a loyal companion. A self-confident, natural, and an un-
spoiled breed.

Bichon Frise: An excellent disposition—a sturdy
animal with a stylish gait—an air of dignity and
intelligence.

Boston Terrier: A well-built dog, clean-cut, not
a fighter but well able to take care of himself—
a gentle disposition—a companion and charming house pet.

Boxer: Beautiful, strong, intelligent, agile—devoted to his master.

Bulldog: A medium-sized dog with a smooth
coat—stability, vigor and strength—good temperament—heavy wrinkles on the head and face
with a low-slung body and massive head.

Bullmastiff: Powerful, a great watchdog, courageous, powerfully built, yet active—fearless yet
docile.

Cairn Terrier: A dog with sporting instincts, short and broad-headed, an active and hardy dog with a foxy expression.

Chihuahua: Intelligent, alert, clannish, does not necessarily like dogs of other breeds, graceful, a swift-moving little dog with a delightful saucy expression.

Chow Chow: A fashionable dog—a guardian—a massive, powerful animal—active and alert—strong muscular dog with perfect balance—a shining coat—a masterpiece of beauty and dignity, but not a dog for everyone.

Cocker Spaniel: Trustworthy, adaptable, sturdy. He is capable of speed and endurance, but sometimes a biter of children. His coat is easy to care for.

Collie: A devoted family dog, an affinity for small children, elegant and beautiful—a guardian.

Dalmatian: Well-known as a firehouse mascot —a retentive memory, dependable and intelligent. Speed, endurance, strength, vitality and fortitude as well as unique markings—a gentleman with

aristocratic bearing. But not a dog for everyone; they do not calm down for many years. I wouldn't recommend this breed for children.

Doberman Pinscher: A noble-looking dog with great muscular power. Alert, agile, temperamental, nimble, and quick. An affectionate, obedient, and loyal dog—quick to defend his master.

English Sheepdog: A homebody, extremely agile, intelligent, affectionate—an ideal house dog. Their coats serve as insulation against heat, cold, and dampness. At home in an apartment or a large home.

English Springer Spaniel: A great hunting dog, wonderful large ears, soft gentle expression, a strong body and a friendly wagging tail—an enthusiastic companion.

Fox Terrier: One of the best known breeds—comes in two varieties, smooth and the wire—strong and wise as well as gay and lively.

German Shepherd: A dog with character, loyal, courageous, with the ability to absorb and retain training—extremely intelligent, patient,

faithful and watchful. A companion, friend, and protector who always wants to please.

Golden Retriever: A powerful looking dog with a kind expression—an active dog appearing eager, alert and self-confident. Bred for retrieving, a loyal animal. A great dog for children.

Great Dane: An elegant giant, noble in appearance, courageous, great endurance, and a powerful dog. He is friendly and dependable, but sometimes overly protective.

Irish Setter: essentially a sporting dog, a lovely looking animal, happy and courageous—full of personality but loves to roam.

Japanese Chin: A toy breed, a good companion, bright and alert. A highbred little dog with a dainty appearance, smart, compact carriage, and profuse coat.

Keeshond: Alert and intelligent, an ideal companion dog—a coat that always looks as if it has just been brushed and trimmed—handsome and well-balanced.

Labrador Retriever: Extremely quick, loves to run and swim—a strong animal. A wonderful dog for children.

Lhasa Apso: Intelligent, quick-hearing, and a finely developed instinct for distinguishing intimates from strangers—keen watchfulness and a hardy, easily trained dog with beautiful dark eyes.

Maltese: Another aristocrat of the dog world—beautiful, intelligent, and lovable—so small they could be carried in ladies' sleeves in times past.

Miniature Schnauzer: Stocky with a wiry coat, abundant whiskers—a hearty, healthy, intelligent breed—fond of children, a charming and delightful family pet.

Papillon: A hardy dog, small, friendly, elegant toy dog of fine-boned structure. They have beautiful butterfly-like ears and an abundant silky coat.

Pekinese: A dignified little dog with an exasperating stubbornness—independent and regal. He is calm and good-tempered, but loves to romp with the family.

Pomeranian: A diminutive dog, docile temperament, sturdy with a vivacious spirit, shows an intelligence in his expression.

Poodle: A coat that lends itself to hair styling, active, intelligent, elegant-appearing dog—well-proportioned—carries himself with an air of distinction and very intelligent.

Pug: A lovable, staunch little dog, requires little coddling, and has a delightful face.

Saint Bernard: Powerful, imposing, strong, and muscular, a keen sense of smell—known for their rescue work, they have saved more than two thousand human lives in the Swiss Alps over three centuries.

Saluki: Some consider this the oldest breed of domesticated dog. Has tremendous speed, able to bring down a gazelle—strong attachment for his master, affectionate and a good watchdog without being aggressive.

Samoyed: Beautiful, strong, gentle, good companion and an excellent watchdog. Never a troublemaker and loyal to its master.

TO THE RESCUE!

Schipperke: Excellent and faithful watchdog—intelligent with a keen expression—rather mischievous, suspicious of strangers—active, agile, indefatigable—kind with children.

Schnauzer: A compact, square-built dog, sturdy, alert, with a stiff wiry coat, bristling eyebrows and whiskers, high-spirited temperament, high intelligence, a reliable dog.

Scottish Terrier: A popular breed—a compact dog, powerful and well-muscled—a keen, sharp, active expression—gives the impression of great power for a small dog.

Siberian husky: Friendly and gentle, sometimes independent, always alert, loves to talk, a great communicator. Traditionally clean and free of body odors—remarkably adaptable with a natural desire to roam—needs an understanding owner.

Weimaraner: An aristocratic dog, medium size —likes being a member of the family, speedy with tremendous endurance, a short, smooth, sleek coat, friendly, alert, and obedient, but not always good for children. Check with the breeder.

Welsh Corgi: A guardian of children, vigilant, intelligent, remarkable speed for its size and shape, alert, watchful, yet friendly—a powerful small dog.

Yorkshire Terrier: A fashionable dog with a long, silky coat—a spirited dog with high head carriage and confident manner.

2

TRAINING YOUR DOG

Does Your Dog Think?

Dogs are like humans—at least to the extent that they require both companionship and mental and physical stimulation. Like the rest of us, Fido responds well to positive rewards and will develop bad habits if bored. Your dog is always learning whether he is undergoing special training or not. Each dog has his own personality and degree of intelligence. A dog is our best friend because he is so willing to live with us humans and to communicate with us.

A dog's logic is different from ours. As a

FIDO LIKES COMFORT.

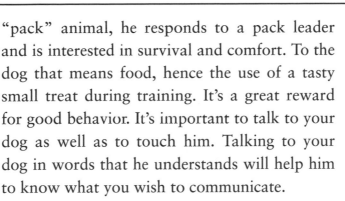

"pack" animal, he responds to a pack leader and is interested in survival and comfort. To the dog that means food, hence the use of a tasty small treat during training. It's a great reward for good behavior. It's important to talk to your dog as well as to touch him. Talking to your dog in words that he understands will help him to know what you wish to communicate.

Fido likes comfort. That's why he will climb onto your sofa whether you are there to cuddle with or not. Some dog owners think this is fine, but if you don't want doggie hair on your sofa, you must find a comfortable place that Fido can call his own.

And how about that intellectual stimulation? He can't read the *Dialogues of Plato,* but he does play with toys, and you need to supply plenty of them for your dog.

Your dog learns with and without your help. If you bring home a new puppy, he has already experienced a number of influences. His mother and littermates have an almost immediate effect on an individual puppy. If mother dog barks to attract attention, that is what the puppies learn. Experiences occurring between three

to twelve weeks of age strongly influence a puppy's behavior.

Socializing Experiences

The best time to acquire a puppy is when it is about eight weeks old. Make sure that little Fido meets as many people as possible. Take your puppy with you in your car to work or to your friends' homes whenever possible. It's also good for your puppy to play with other dogs and children. All this helps to ensure that Fido will have good socializing experiences and will grow up to be a happy and social dog.

Dogs lacking in these social experiences can be more difficult to train. But once the dog gets to know you and his name, he can still be trained in an hour or less. It's difficult to know exactly what experiences your puppy has had before he is eight weeks old. If you purchase your puppy from a breeder, attempt to find out as much as possible about his early experiences. The more a puppy has been handled, the more likely he is to respond well to training. It is usually best to avoid purchasing your puppy from a pet store. These dogs can have more health

problems, and most are deprived of the necessary socialization that can make training more difficult. Again, your local pet shelter is a great place to get your dog.

*Fido Speaks Dogese
or Another Foreign Tongue*

Dr. Doolittle had it right. He could understand dog language and so can you. But you must pay close attention. Fido "speaks" body language. He will tell you when he wants to go outside, when he's hungry, and when he's thirsty. He will tell you when he wants to walk and when he wants to take a ride. And very importantly, he will sit and cock his head and tell you he hasn't a clue about what you're talking about.

When someone comes to your door whom he doesn't like, he may growl or snarl. Then you'd better stop and listen because a dog's instincts are to be reckoned with. Dogs can often tell what people are like. Animals in the wild have to go by their instincts regarding who's friendly and who's not, so they know a lot more than we can easily observe.

A dog's ears also tell you a lot about what he is thinking and feeling. When he is upset, his ears move close to his head. When he is trying to hear something, his ears stand straight up.

When a dog's tail goes between his legs, he's scared. When he's happy, it's wagging. If a dog's tail goes straight up and his back goes up, watch out. Your dog may be ready to attack something or somebody.

I have dogs that like to bring their leash over to me when it's time to take a walk. I had a Neapolitan mastiff that liked to walk over to me and put his large mouth around my wrist and lead me to where he wanted me to go. He would take me to his toys to play, to the front door to take me outside. Now that's body language! You've heard the story, "Where does a gorilla sit? Anywhere he wants to!"

Your Dog's Vocabulary

Perhaps the most important concept in training your dog can be summed up in one word—consistency. If you're consistent you'll be able to train your dog to come to you every time, sit every time, stay every time, lie down

every time, and many other things in just one hour or less. But it won't work unless you're consistent! When you communicate with your dog and expect your dog to obey, use only two words. Your dog doesn't understand theories or philosophy; he won't read that treatise, just chew on it. But he can understand two words, providing he hears them in the right order. Always start by saying your dog's name. Do this always. You will get your dog's attention and then follow it with a one word command like this:

"Fido, come."

"Fido, sit."

"Fido, stay."

Please, not all at one time. Start with the first command, "Fido, come," and stay with that command until you have achieved success. It shouldn't take too long. If you start with three different commands, you might as well give Fido a book of instructions—in Sanskrit. If you reverse the order ("Come, Fido"), your dog will hear his name but miss the command. Remember, consistency, consistency, consistency. If you begin with your dog's name and then issue

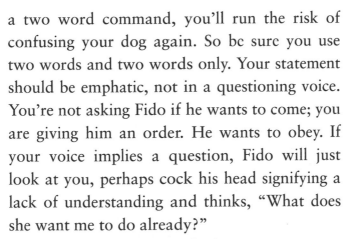

a two word command, you'll run the risk of confusing your dog again. So be sure you use two words and two words only. Your statement should be emphatic, not in a questioning voice. You're not asking Fido if he wants to come; you are giving him an order. He wants to obey. If your voice implies a question, Fido will just look at you, perhaps cock his head signifying a lack of understanding and thinks, "What does she want me to do already?"

Whenever possible, look into your pet's eyes when giving a command. Of course you can't if Fido is out of sight. If he can see you but has no eye contact, the command can fail. Have you ever gone to the veterinarian and Fido puts his head under your arm? He is feeling that if he can't see the doctor, then the doctor can't see him! The same thing happens when training your dog. If Fido can't see you, you can't see him—and he then feels that he doesn't have to mind you.

With two word communication you will succeed in training your dog in one hour or less. I'm not talking about an hour on Monday and an hour on Tuesday; I'm talking about one hour

WHENEVER POSSIBLE, LOOK INTO YOUR PET'S EYE WHEN GIVING A COMMAND.

total time. After you read these directions or watch my videos, your dog will learn these simple commands by the end of one hour. If after completing this simple learning process, you want to train Fido to go to the refrigerator and take out a beer, open the can, pour its contents into a glass, and bring it to you on a tray, your dog will need the more advanced course.

Now that we have trained you to use only two words beginning with your dog's name, you need to learn how important body language is to your dog's understanding. While you are telling your dog to come ("Fido, Come; Fido, Come"), you'll want to use lots of body language. Let your dog know exactly where you want him to come to. Raise your hand up toward the sky or ceiling and propel your hand toward the ground as you say, "Fido, Come." If you want your dog to sit, then you use the palm of your hand to show the dog that he must back down on his haunches while you say, "Fido, Sit." If you want your dog to lie down, you can say "Fido, Lay." If your dog understands the difference between transitive and intransitive verbs, you might say, "Fido, Lie." It's equally

SOME THINGS TAKE MORE THAN
AN HOUR TO LEARN.

possible to say, "Fido, Down." You can use the same word if Fido is jumping on you. Dogs seem to be able to understand the two meanings. But use as much body language as you can. Also use your eyes, providing your dog is close to you. If Fido is across the street, forget about eye contact.

Sometimes your dog will intentionally not look at you. Dogs, like children or our mates, don't always want to be told what to do. So you will need to try to get your dog's attention, and eye contact is important. Say his name a little stronger, clap your hands—one or the other will cause your dog to look at you.

Control That Impulse

More than occasionally, we lose patience. There are times when we want to strike out at that uncooperative, dense, four-legged creature that we have only recently acquired. But control that impulse. You will accomplish nothing by hitting your dog, at least nothing of a positive nature. Hitting your dog can make him frightened of you. He won't behave or learn any more readily because the odds are good he didn't

FIDO, LAY.

understand what you wanted. When your dog doesn't understand you, it's your fault, not the dog's. So resist that temptation to strike your dog. That's important—so important I'll probably say it several more times in the course of this book.

If your dog has soiled the floor, or perhaps left a little surprise behind your Christmas tree, do not put his nose in it. When a dog finds another dog's surprise out in the street, the first thing your dog will do is to put his nose in it. So if you do this with his own "accidents," you're not teaching him anything. But we'll get around to potty training your dog a little later.

Positive Reinforcement

Positive reinforcement is vital in dog training. People respond better with positive reinforcement also. Remember when you were in the kindergarten or first grade and you brought home a paper with a little happy face. I ran home as fast as I could so Mummy and Daddy could see my gold star. Make your dog understand that he is a good dog, a very good dog, and reinforce with vigorous petting and verbal

NEVER, NEVER HIT YOUR DOG.

compliments. Your dog is in your home to make you happy, not to make you miserable. If your dog only makes you miserable, then you are not communicating well with Fido.

When should you start to train your dog? The ideal age is twelve weeks old, but it does no harm if you wish to begin training at eight weeks. Like the education of children, growth and development are important to animals as well.

Dogs, like children, like treats. Find out what your dog likes, maybe a dog biscuit. Get a plastic bag and break up a dog biscuit into small pieces. When Fido does what you want him to do, during the first ten or fifteen minutes of the training session, reward him with a treat. Accompanying the treat should be your enthusiastic response to his success.

The adult person in the family who is closest to the dog should do the initial training. Once you are well on the way to an obedient dog, other members of the family may assist with the training.

Teaching Your Dog to Come

First, you need to be armed with dog goodies.

POSITIVE REINFORCEMENT REALLY HELPS WHEN TRAINING YOUR DOG.

I've had people walk around with pieces of cheese, spaghetti, rice, one little piece of chicken, whatever your dog likes. Be careful, though. The title of this book is not, "How To Make Your Dog Fat in One Hour." Fido will be very happy if you give him just a teeny weeny piece.

You are now in your living room or out in the backyard. Fido is happily running around, sniffing everything in sight and a few things not in sight. You are standing expectantly at one place in your room or yard. Raise your hand toward the sky, attempt to get some eye contact with Fido, and say loudly and with authority, "Fido, Come." Your arm forcefully moves toward the ground in front of you. Let's assume that nothing happens. Fido is still happily prancing around the yard. So you try it again. No luck this time either. You begin to feel foolish wondering whether the neighbors are watching. Suppose this fails five or six times. Slowly walk over to Fido, pick up his collar like you are picking up a feather and walk back over to where you were standing. The second you get back to where you were standing, you should now get excited and tell your dog: "Fido, Good;

Fido, Good; Fido, Good," followed by a very small piece of his favorite treat. We then repeat the lesson. When Fido responds correctly the first time, we repeat a very strong "Fido, Good; Fido Good." Again, the second he gets to you, you need to become very excited and let him know how happy you are. Again, you repeat, "Fido, Good; Fido, Good; Fido, Good." What you say is just as important and later more so than the treat. I've never had a dog yet that has not come over to the owner at least after the owner walked over and led him back by the collar and then telling the dog how good he was accompanied by the dog's favorite treat. Once you have your dog coming over to you, you should repeat the lesson eight to ten times. You don't have to continue giving your dog treats— only during the first fifteen or twenty minutes of the lesson. Remember, dogs, like people, need their good work complimented.

Once when I was giving a group lesson, a puppy seemed not to understand what was expected of him. He would not come after a number of repetitions. An older dog, watching my frustration from the sidelines, walked over to

the puppy, picked him up by the neck, and brought him over to me. I handed the dog a dollar.

Training Your Dog to Sit

This is a simple command for most dogs to learn. Simply walk over to the dog, pick up his collar, like you're picking up a feather, press down on his rear like you're pushing down on a feather, accompanied with a very strong, "Fido, Sit." That's all there is to it. But as soon as you do that, you must make a very big deal out of it saying, "Fido, Good; Fido, Good; Fido, Good." He probably won't know what he has done to merit such praise the first time he performs successfully. So you need to do the same thing again. Each time the process should get easier. Fido should require less and less pushing on his rear, and soon Fido will sit in response to the words and hand signals alone. For this training pull your elbow back to your rib cage, then make a circular motion down toward the floor. It may take eight or ten repetitions to get this response from Fido. But never forget to let him know how happy you are that he's doing what you want.

How long can your dog concentrate at your school of higher learning? Only ten minutes at a time. At the end of a ten minute period, allow Fido to play freely for two or three minutes before resuming the instruction.

Teaching Your Dog to Lie Down

Getting your dog to lie down is very important. You now have your dog coming to you. He now sits down also. And he does these things every single time. Getting your dog to lie down is one of the simplest of all the commands. First call your dog over to you. You commend him for doing so saying: "Fido, Good; Fido, Good." Then follow that with "Fido, Sit. Fido, Good; Fido, Good." Then say, "Fido, Down." At the same time pat your hand down on the ground. Pat right in front of you, and Fido will just pick up his front feet and fall down. When Fido responds, don't forget to praise him extravagantly. Very occasionally it may be necessary to pick up his front legs and lay them on the ground. At the same time you say, "Fido, Down."

Getting Your Dog to Stay

You have now gotten your dog to come, sit, and lie down. Now you will want Fido to stay, a more difficult idea to your dog. After all, if you were a puppy or a young dog, would you want to stay in one place. It's more fun to run around, either the house, yard, or especially down to the local elementary school where there are children to jump on. No, your dog has to learn to "stay." Pull your elbow back toward your rib cage and point your finger out at the dog while you say, with great emphasis, "Fido, Stay; Fido, Stay." Use your gruff, growling voice, "Fido, Stay." Let Fido know who's boss. Say this at least three times. Maintain eye contact. Stay exactly where you are. Tell your dog, "Fido, Stay," even if he is only six inches from you.

Dogs hate to stay. It's one of the toughest things to teach. You almost have to talk to Fido in his own language. A growling voice communicates animal dominance and gets their attention.

Tell him how good he is that he "stayed" during that period, even though only a few

SOME PUPPIES HAVE
A LONG LEARNING CURVE.

seconds. Do this three or four times before you take two steps back. Do not attempt to go back more than a few steps on the first day. On the second day, you usually can go back a few more steps.

Potty Training

Unfortunately, I cannot guarantee success with potty training in one hour or less! But it usually can be done in about twenty-four hours or less. If your dog has left a little surprise on your floor, grab a couple of paper towels, go over to the spot, put your hand next to the spot, and hit your hand with a very strong, "Fido No; Fido, No." Again, hit your hand, not the dog. Mop it up, pick up a little teeny bit with the paper towel, walk outside with your dog and put the paper towel where you want your dog to go. Then turn around, just as if he put it there all by himself, and then tell him, "Fido, Good; Fido, Good." Act excited even though you're the one who put the paper towel there. The first time you see your dog going outside all by himself, you should run outside, jump up and down, and act really excited. Let your dog

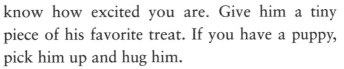

know how excited you are. Give him a tiny piece of his favorite treat. If you have a puppy, pick him up and hug him.

Remember, if your dog relieves himself in your house, you must show your displeasure. If you find a little surprise the next morning, don't believe your dog has forgotten. Dogs and elephants never forget. But only a few of us keep elephants in our bedrooms. If you do, you're probably not reading this book.

Remember that nice pair of socks so beautifully folded that your puppy found last year. Ripping it up was the greatest fun he'd had since he found Dad's slippers three weeks earlier. You took the socks away from him, properly admonished him for his transgression, and put the socks back in the drawer. When you got back from vacation, your dog went to the drawer hoping to find the socks. No, ma'am, dogs don't forget. But happily, they want to please you. So give them a toy so they are not tempted to chew either socks or slippers. Love them dearly when they behave properly.

When potty training your dog, be consistent, be strong, and be vigilant. Don't worry what your

neighbors will think if they see you dancing around happily with your puppy after he does his business.

I know that some trainers use crates to potty train. I'm not one of them. But crates are okay when you're using a doggy door. Place the crate immediately inside the doggy door so your dog can leave the house to go outside, but when he comes back in, he must go directly into the crate. This works best when you are not at home during the day. Fido will not be able to tear your house apart while you're at work. It's cruel to lock your dog in a crate for hours when you're not at home, only to keep Fido from relieving himself. If he has a dog door in front of him, he has more freedom to be a dog. Dog doors are wonderful, perhaps the greatest invention for dogs. I have two of them, and they're easy to install. If you're renting a house and it's not appropriate to damage a door, remove one of the doors, usually the back door. Purchase a used door of the same size, and install a doggy door at the bottom. When you are ready to move out of your rental, reinstall the original door.

If you have a condominium and live on the

thirty-fifth floor, perhaps you have a balcony or ledge. Purchase a small children's swimming pool, fill it with dirt, plant some grass seed (and a few weeds), and your dog has a perfect potty when you're away. A doggy door leading to his restroom makes a perfect exit and entrance. There may be room for Fido to lie out in the sun while he waits for you to come home. Check the width of your safety railing, however. If your small dog can crawl through, I wouldn't sell him life insurance.

Do You Have More Than One Dog?

If you have more than one dog, be sure that you give your command to one dog at a time. You never want to say, "Fido, Spot, come." That's a good way to confuse both dogs. Remember, the name of the dog first, then the command. I have six dogs. When I get ready to leave, they each, in turn, receive a command to "sit." If I want to take one of the dogs with me, I call that dog over to me while the others remain sitting. With good training you will be able to open your front door, either leave or enjoy the fresh air, and you will have no fear

that your dog or dogs will escape into the wild blue yonder. You want to have control over them, and the only way you can do so is through consistent communication.

If you need to train more than one dog, be sure that you work only with one dog at a time. Place the other dog or dogs out of sight, perhaps in the next room.

Preserving Your Space

Sometimes you come home from work tired. You need and deserve your rest. After all, you've been working hard all day. You love your dog or dogs just as I love my six dogs. But there are times I need my space, and I suspect there are times when you need your space also. But what to do? Your dog loves you and expects to nuzzle close to you, especially when you're lying down. You'll need to communicate to your dog that you would rather not have his company at present. Pull your elbow back toward your ribcage and with a swift motion of your hand and finger say a very strong, "Fido, Go; Fido, Go." Even if Fido takes only one step back, he's got the idea. Now don't let Fido creep

back toward you, so before you know it he's resting his lovable head on your arm and drooling into your newly-washed hand that you've reserved for turning pages of your favorite novel and for nibbling human treats. No, Fido must learn to respect your space. Fido has those moments too when he wants to be alone. It's good to respect those moments also.

Begging from the Table

I don't feed my dogs at the table. I never have nor do I ever plan to in the future. I don't want my dogs begging so by not feeding them from the table, they don't beg. At the same time if I'm eating popcorn or walking around eating a bag of potato chips (well, at least some potato chips, not the whole bag!) I don't drop them for my dogs to eat because I call this "begging" too.

If your dog begs, you can train him not to. Merely repeat my previous training procedure: Pull your arm back toward your rib cage and point straight out and say, "Fido, Go; Fido, Go." These are my words, and, of course, my dogs have learned to understand them. You can use any expression you wish. You must be

consistent, however, and always use the same words to designate the same meaning.

If you do want to give your table scraps to your dog, save them in the refrigerator and give them to your dog a couple of hours later or the next day. In this way Fido won't associate the table scraps with your meal. If you give your dog the scraps immediately after your meal, he will come to expect these treats and the vicious circle of begging will start all over again.

Your Home Can Disappear, or Your Dog
Likes to Chew on Your Furniture

If your dog (usually a puppy) chews on your furniture, that's pretty serious. We see lots of dogs in animal shelters because of such damage. Dogs need to be taught that your furniture is not theirs. First, understand that dogs, like children, need lots and lots of toys. It's good to have a box just for their toys. You don't need to spend much money; your dog hasn't studied economics and knows nothing of the value of money. But whatever is in the box belongs to your dog. Rope with knots in it is a good toy, also the cutoff legs of an old pair of jeans with a

big knot in the knee (Please, not the whole pair. Your dog will get the wrong idea and go to your closet next.), or used stuffed animals are a dog's favorite. Second-hand stores are a good place to purchase dog toys at a reasonable cost. My four Greyhounds believe that stuffed animals were made for them and them only.

Let's assume that your dog has started chewing your couch. Bring your dog over to the couch. Hit your own hand loudly so your dog hears the sound while you say, "Fido, No; Fido, No; Fido, No." Don't hurt your hand but clap like you were applauding. Then turn around and take one of his toys and put it into his mouth and say, "Fido, Good; Fido, Good; Fido, Good." Then give Fido another of his toys and repeat the above, "Fido, Good; Fido, Good; Fido, Good." This can be repeated with three or four toys, but only one at a time. I don't care how angry you are. Now wait fifteen or twenty minutes. Go back over to your couch. He most likely hasn't touched it. After all, you're home now. Now you need to make a big deal that Fido hasn't touched your couch. You are enormously happy. Turn that negative that you've

been using into lots and lots of positive.

Quite regularly people tell me that their dog chewed up their favorite pair of shoes. Sometimes it's their purse. "What should I do?" they ask. A dog's imagination seems endless when it comes to chewing things around the house. You have to remember to give Fido his own toys to play with and to teach him to play only with his own toys.

Your shoes and your purse smell a lot like you to your dog. The easiest thing to do is to pick them up! Don't leave them around for your dog to discover and to think they're his toys.

The procedure is the same as with your furniture. If you find that your dog chewed a favorite shoe, put your hand on the shoe and hit your hand accompanied with a very strong, "Fido, No; Fido, No; Fido, No." And as we have already said, give Fido one of his own toys and say, "Fido, Good; Fido, Good; Fido, Good." Wait about ten minutes. He probably hasn't touched those shoes because you're home now. Go over to him and tell him how good he is. Remember—positive communication, not negative.

DOGS LIKE TO DIG.

Does Your Dog Dig in Your Garden?

If you love to garden, nothing can be more aggravating than to find holes in your garden and your lovely flowers dug up and strewn around the yard. If you want a garden and a dog, you'll need to teach Fido some better manners. Most dogs love to dig. On cold days, dogs can lie next to the ground for warmth. On warm days, dogs get the opposite effect; they experience the coolness of the newly dug earth.

To break your dog from digging, take your dog over to the hole he has dug. Put your hand next to the hole and again hit your hand accompanied with a very strong, "Fido, No; Fido, No, Fido, No." Let him know that this behavior is not acceptable. Now you must have some outdoor toys for Fido, and this is the time to give him a toy—just as you did when Fido chewed your Louis XIV sofa. When Fido has his toy in his mouth, you repeat, "Fido, Good; Fido, Good; Fido, Good." Just as you did with the sofa transgression, wait around for ten to fifteen minutes. Make sure that Fido has not resumed his digging during that time and then begin the

positive reinforcement: "Fido, Good; Fido, Good; Fido, Good," with other strong signs of love.

The Barker Stopper®

A device I've used successfully to help condition my dogs to stop barking and a device also useful to get your dog to stop digging is the "Barker Stopper." The device is no more than a small electronic instrument that will emit a loud, high-pitched sound. When your dog barks without a good reason, or digs a hole in your flower garden, press the button on the Barker Stopper while admonishing Fido as previously described: "Fido, No; Fido, No; Fido, No." Soon Fido will be conditioned to the sound of the Barker Stopper, and he will know when he hears the sound that barking and/or digging is not approved. Don't use it to call your dog, however, or for commands, such as come, sit, lie down, etc. You can use it for a menu of other unwanted behaviors, such as chewing, jumping, digging, or chasing cats. There is also the "Super Barker Stopper®" that goes off automatically and works even if you're not there. It can be mounted on a tree or fence and has a built-in

microphone that sets off the sound every time your dog barks. Once the behavior stops the Super Barker Stopper then resets itself and is ready for the next bark.

How About a Choke Collar?

I know that many trainers use them. But I think they're terrible! If you have one, I'd throw it away. All they teach your dog is to be choked! I wouldn't want somebody putting a choke collar on me to teach me something. If you use the proven method I've described here, you won't need a choke collar, and your dog will be a much happier pooch.

But Fido does need a collar so you can take him for a walk and to hold his various identification and vaccination tags. Many dogs take a little time to get used to a collar. They are frightened of it, and it drives them crazy. If Fido rebels, put his collar on for just a few minutes, then take it off. Let him know it won't hurt him. Leave it on a little bit longer the next time. In a couple of days you should be able to leave his collar on.

Do the same thing with his leash. Frightened dogs can just lie down and not move. Fido needs time to adjust to this new and strange world. Like his collar, start with a few minutes at a time. Soon Fido will identify his leash with going for a walk—usually a joyful time of the day for Fido.

I use a product called the Happy "Walker®." It helps you train your dog not to pull on his leash. You place the small, 2½ inch unit over the dog's leash. When Fido pulls on his leash, the device emits a loud, high-pitched sound. That sound accompanied by his master's firm admonition to behave, acts as a great training device. And it doesn't hurt Fido.

Listen To That Thunder

If you have a dog who is afraid of thunder and lightning, go to your favorite music store and find a CD or cassette of storm sounds. Play it very softly at first while you are at home and continue with your daily routine. Do not console your dog in any way. Consoling him sends a message that there is a problem and he should be alarmed. Over the period of a few

days, increase the volume level gradually until it reaches the level of a real storm. Do this every once in a while until Fido is no longer frightened of a storm.

Important Command Tips

- Work with your dog for a ten minute period, then let him relax for a while before continuing the training.

- Work with only one dog at a time. Keep other dogs elsewhere so they don't distract the one in training.

- Use treats to reinforce training.

- Let your dog know how happy and pleased you are when he does what you want him to do. For every "no" used, there should be ten "Fido Good" reinforcements. Your dog wants to please you.

- If your dog is cocking his head or not responding, he does not understand what you want. Repeat the command.

- Eye contact is imperative to train your dog.

- Never hit your dog for any reason.

POSITIVE TRAINING
IS SUCCESSFUL TRAINING

3

GENERAL CARE
OF YOUR DOG

To Bathe or Not To Bathe,
That is the Question

Some people want to give their dogs a bath once a month, some once a week. But most dogs clean themselves and require a bath only occasionally. Sometimes Fido will really smell doggy or a little musty. Then it's okay to give him a bath. But don't just give Fido a bath for no reason. Too many baths can make your dog's skin very dry; they're just not very good for your dog. But if you are going to give Fido a

bath, be sure to get a good doggy shampoo. Check with your pet store and/or your vet.

Sometimes a dog will be afraid of the water and won't want to take a bath. In such a situation you must approach the bath idea slowly. Use only a damp sponge the first day and let him get used to having a little water on him. Increase the water slowly until he gets accustomed to a little water dripping down his body. At this point he should be ready for his bath.

If you're bathing a puppy, pick a comfortable warm day. Use a good doggy shampoo with warm, not hot water. When you're through washing, rinse out the shampoo thoroughly, then make sure he's well-dried. If the day is warm, Fido can shake off the excess moisture outside in your yard.

Yes, Virginia, Your Dog Loves to Eat

Puppies need a little different kind of food than older dogs. Before you run out to purchase your dog, be sure you can afford to feed him properly. Your dog's nutrition depends on his size, age, health, breed, and lifestyle. A quiet dog can develop behavioral problems if fed the

same thing as an energetic dog. If you have a "working" dog, he needs extra nutrition and some extra protein. If Fido is a puppy, he will require more calories than an adult dog. Dogs like eating new foods, but be careful because catering to your dog in this way could make him a finicky eater. Also, feeding Fido new foods can cause diarrhea and gas.

New foods do not include tinsel from Christmas trees or chocolate that you eat daily. A box of chocolates can kill your dog, and so can eating tinsel. Dog owners should be aware of such poisons before your dog gets himself into serious trouble. Make sure you have enough toys for Fido so he won't be tempted to mutilate his digestive system with tinsel. If you have a new puppy, you must be especially vigilant.

And be careful at Thanksgiving. We all love that turkey and dressing, but too much turkey given to your dog can cause Pancreatitis, a serious disorder. A tablespoon of turkey and a teaspoon of dressing are plenty for Fido.

I knew a Golden Retriever who was trained to stay away from turkeys and chickens on a farm. He managed to do this providing the

birds didn't get near *his* food. When a turkey got near his food, he tried growling and barking but to no avail. Finally, he went over to the turkey, opened his mouth wide, and put it over the turkey's head. I guess that dog never bit the turkey's head off. Maybe he knew it wasn't good for him. But that turkey never went near the dog's food again!

If your dog is sick and not eating too well, try one pound of hamburger, boiled and drained. Don't add salt or pepper. Do add one cup of Minute Rice (or a substitute), mix together and feed small amounts to Fido. You can also add a tablespoon of cottage cheese (dogs love it). It will help him get well.

You can also stir some regular dry dog food with water and a couple of eggs. Let it all soak until the water and eggs are absorbed. Make little patties, bake at 325 degrees for 20 minutes. Give your dog little bites of it.

If your dog spends a lot of time outdoors in the winter, that means he will probably need extra food. Fido will seem hungrier, so be sensitive to his needs; it's okay to give him a little extra food under those conditions.

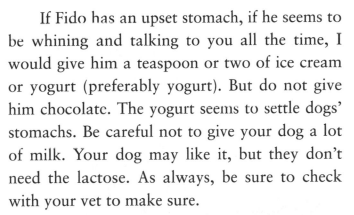

If Fido has an upset stomach, if he seems to be whining and talking to you all the time, I would give him a teaspoon or two of ice cream or yogurt (preferably yogurt). But do not give him chocolate. The yogurt seems to settle dogs' stomachs. Be careful not to give your dog a lot of milk. Your dog may like it, but they don't need the lactose. As always, be sure to check with your vet to make sure.

My Greyhounds just love apples, grapefruit, bananas, strawberries, about any fruit you can imagine. I give them at least one serving in the morning and one at night. Be careful with onions, however, since they can cause anemia in dogs by destroying their red blood cells.

I knew a dog named Holly who was only a few weeks old. She wouldn't eat. Her master hired a housesitter whose job it was to feed Holly. The girl became very frustrated when Holly refused her food. Soon the sitter started feeding Holly with a spoon. This seemed to work. Holly started to gain a little weight, and when her master came home, she was delighted that Holly was eating. But she was less than happy to learn that she would have to feed

Holly on her lap with a spoon! Thank goodness Holly hadn't learned to use chopsticks.

Make sure your dog has lots of water. In case you're snowed in and can't get home at night, be sure there is plenty of water for your dog. Water makes up 60 percent of an adult dog's body, and the percentage is even higher for puppies. His body loses water through urination, defecation, and panting. If you're going on a trip, be sure to have enough water for your dog. Take water from home and mix it with "new" water. Changing the water supply completely and suddenly can make a dog sick. I often take a sealed bag filled with water. It works great when on a hike too. I have a backpack for my dogs, who can then carry their own water and supplies.

Don't give Fido just table scraps. If Fido is a puppy, you will want to feed him a food formula designed for puppies and their less mature digestive systems. If you have an older dog, you'll need to cut down on his protein and give him a dog food designed for doggie senior citizens. Your vet will offer good advice on what's best for your dog. By the time Fido is a year old,

he will need only one or two feedings a day. You can feed him at regular times or when you feel like it. But it is not a good idea to feed Fido immediately before or immediately after exercising, or before a trip.

We humans like variety in our food, but dogs are not that fussy. Fido will like the same food day after day. Interestingly enough, if you decide to give Fido a variety of foods, he is likely to become confused about what he wants to eat and may develop a disdain for anything you spoon into his dish. So don't create a fussy eater; give Fido the same great food every day.

A Place for Fido to Sleep

Comfort is important to dogs as well as to people. Make sure that Fido's bed is large enough for him to stretch out completely. Watch for drafty areas. Fido may not complain, but it's our responsibility to find a location where the temperature is reasonably even—neither too hot nor too cold. You will want to find materials for his bed that are washable. After all, cleanliness is important to you and, hopefully, to Fido also.

A Health Club for Fido

No, Fido doesn't need to pay dues for a health club just to get his exercise. Monthly dues are just for us humans. But your dog does need exercise. You would think that your dog would get enough exercise just being a dog, but unfortunately that is not the case. Frequent walks are wonderful for your dog (and for you too). It's great if you are a marathon runner, but Fido may have to work up to that ten mile run. But whatever you do, don't just put your dog outside and expect him to exercise. Dogs react like many people we all know; they will sit happily in the sun and move as little as possible. I have lots of land where I live in the mountains. My dogs could run for miles if they wanted to. But they will only run when I'm with them. I walk with them through snow, sleet, and hail. It's good for me and good for them!

And don't forget hot weather problems with your dog. Dogs don't sweat the way humans do. They sweat a little between their toes and they pant. So you must make sure that your dog has enough water, particularly on hot days. Running water into a pan is best.

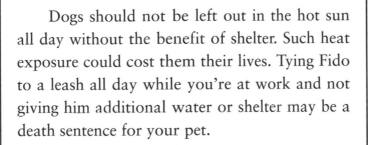

Dogs should not be left out in the hot sun all day without the benefit of shelter. Such heat exposure could cost them their lives. Tying Fido to a leash all day while you're at work and not giving him additional water or shelter may be a death sentence for your pet.

Those Nails Are Just Too Long

Dogs will sometimes just let you go ahead and cut their nails. You should be so lucky! Some dogs even cut their own nails. No, they don't sit there and use nail clippers, but some will just bite off their overgrown nails. As you already know, I have a Neapolitan Mastiff. Sometimes, from the next room, I hear a crunch, crunch, crunch. Yes, it's Bull biting his nails. Most of the time, however, it's necessary for Fido's master to cut his nails. Is Fido happy about this? Usually not.

But we can make this easier, not only for your dog but for ourselves. First, get some doggy clippers from your pet store or vet. For the first day, merely touch Fido's toes with the clippers. Don't try to cut anything. Do this several times. Maybe on the third day, cut one nail.

On the fourth day, cut two nails. In other words, get your dog used to the clippers very slowly. That will avoid a trauma to your dog and to you.

Brushing Those Fangs

Dogs need to brush their teeth. Unfortunately, they can't do it themselves. You can purchase special toothbrushes for Fido from your pet store or veterinarian. But you should not use human toothpaste. Get a toothpaste designed for dogs, and brush daily or weekly. Be sure to have your vet check Fido's teeth when you take him for his annual or semiannual checkup. He may need to have a tooth pulled just like people. Dogs can also get an abscessed tooth that can be very painful.

Does Fido Need a Beauty Shop?

One of my dogs is a Golden Retriever/Chow. He's an absolute sweetheart, but he has very long hair. So he's always extremely hot even though I live in the mountains where it's ordinarily quite cool. This dog is always panting, so I get him groomed once every two to

four months. When he's done, he has very short hair, which makes him very, very happy.

If you have a dog who's not used to being groomed, you will need to make a really big deal out of it. Let Fido know how gorgeous he is. Tell him this even if he really looks funny. Tell him how proud you are of his new haircut. Tell him how handsome he looks. That's what it takes to make a happy dog.

Grooming sessions develop a bond between dog and owner when it's done right and will sometimes make your dog much more pleasant to live with. Not only will it make him feel good, it will help to keep his skin and coat healthy, eliminating loose hair and dirt as well as toning his muscles. Puppies don't need much grooming, but it's good to introduce your puppy to personal care a bit at a time. Obtain a good quality brush, a steel comb, and a "hand mitt" or glove. Use your tools gently.

Whether you should pay big bucks to groom your dog is your decision. Unless there is a matter of health, your dog's ego is not wedded to his appearance. If yours is, and your pocketbook can afford it, go for it.

Brownie is a Social Animal

If you acquire a new puppy, try to allow her to interact with people as much as possible. Take your dog with you to as many places as you can; she will bond with you more quickly and learn how to get along with other people. Such experiences will also make the training process easier.

My dogs look forward to going to the bank with me. I have a van that's just for my dogs; it's a huge one-ton van filled with pillows and blankets. When I want to take all my dogs at one time, we all jump in the van, and there's a place for everybody. When we arrive at the bank, the dogs all put their heads out the windows so they can each receive a complimentary dog biscuit. And to think we used to get lollipops!

Some dogs get very nervous when traveling in a car. Some shake and tremble and are just scared to death. Most of the time Fido gets over his nervousness. But you can help matters along. Put your nervous dog in the car and drive just a short distance, perhaps to the post office and back. Or take him just a few blocks and

return home. Try to make the trip fun for Fido. Let him know that everything is okay. Drive him to the park every day for a week where you play ball with him. With repeated experiences that are fun for the dog, his nervousness should go away. Most dogs simply love car trips, but some must approach them gradually and with patience. Patience, of course, is important in training and bonding with any dog.

Many times Brownie will be suspicious of strangers, such as postmen or delivery people. The postman can make friends with Brownie by bringing her a dog biscuit or treat. My postman brings my Greyhound an apple, so my dog loves him to death. Have your postman bring the mail to the house with a dog biscuit tied to the mail with a rubber band. Your dog will love the postman and no federal postal regulations will have been breached.

If you get a dog and just put it out in the backyard, tie him up, and then expect him to come into the house once in a while when there is a stranger there, let me tell you, that can make him a very effective guard dog. Be sure that is what you want before you induce that kind of

behavior in your dog. If you are tying your dog up in the backyard, think about giving your dog to somebody who can give it a good home.

A Dog Door—One of Your Best Investments

I hear from people all the time telling me how bad they feel because they have to leave their dogs alone eight to twelve hours a day. With all the working people today, all working as hard as possible trying to earn enough money to buy dog food, there's a lot more traffic, and it just seems that it takes longer to get home. Poor Fido is alone, no one to play with, and no one to talk to. And this goes on five to six days a week. A remedy is on the way. Get that dog door that will allow Fido to go in and out of the house at will. Even if you have to put a (heaven forbid) crate by the dog door to prevent doggie access to the rest of your house, Fido will still be able to go outside to your nice fenced-in yard, and when he needs to retreat from the elements, he can re-enter the house and into the crate to nap. After all, you wouldn't want to be locked in a small area all day, and neither does Fido.

4

FIRST AID FOR YOUR PET

First aid is not a substitute for veterinary treatment. But in an emergency, your knowledge of first aid for your dog is vital. After giving your dog first aid, however, always plan to take him to a vet as soon as possible. Here are a few of the many problems your dog can experience.

Bite Wounds from Another Dog

Approach your dog carefully to avoid getting bitten yourself. Wash the wound with soap and water and check to see if the wound requires stitches. If it does, take your dog to the vet as soon as possible. If not, Neosporin® or

Bacitracin may be used to stop an infection, a common result of puncture wounds.

Bleeding

Apply firm, direct pressure over the bleeding area until the bleeding stops. Avoid bandages that can cut off circulation. Call your veterinarian immediately.

If Your Pet Stops Breathing

Check to see if your dog is choking on a foreign object. If an object is removed from his throat and the animal is still not breathing, place the animal with its right side down. Close the animal's mouth and exhale directly into his nose (not his mouth) until the chest expands. Cover the dog's nose with a handkerchief or a thin cloth. Exhale twelve to fifteen times per minute (or once every four to five seconds). At the same time, apply heart massage with the other hand. (Your dog's heart is located in the lower half of the chest behind the elbow of the front leg.) Place your hand over the heart and compress the chest one to two inches for large

animals, one inch for small animals. Apply heart massage seventy to ninety times per minute. Call your veterinarian immediately.

Burns (Chemical, Electrical, and Heat)

Watch for singed hair, blistering, swelling, or redness of the skin. Flush the burn area immediately with large amounts of cold water. Apply an ice pack for fifteen to twenty minutes. Call your veterinarian immediately.

Poisoning

This category includes vomiting, convulsions, diarrhea, salivation, weakness, depression, and pain.

Write down what your pet ingested and how much. Immediately, call your veterinarian or poison control center. Do not induce vomiting or attempt treatment without direction from the doctor. In case of poisoning on the skin or fur from oils, paints, or chemicals, wash the animal with mild soap and rinse well. As with all medical problems with your dog, call your veterinarian.

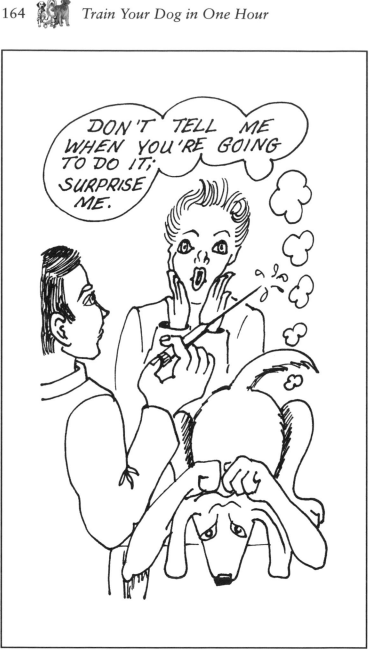

Foreign Object Embedded in Your Dog

Porcupine quills are sharp, hollow shafts. They should be extracted with care. Some vets suggest only doing this with anesthesia. Foxtails are a barbed seed sometimes visible in the eye, nose, mouth, throat or skin of your dog and cause severe irritation. Foxtails are usually too deep to remove without general anesthetic. Call your veterinarian.

Heat Stroke

Symptoms are rapid or difficulty breathing, vomiting, high body temperature, collapse. Place the animal in a tub of cold water or gently soak with a garden hose, or wrap in a cold, wet towel. Call your veterinarian immediately.

Insect Bites

Symptoms include singed hair, blistering, swelling, or redness of the skin.

Remove the stinger and apply cold packs. If isolated from veterinary care, a topical cortisone or an anti-inflammatory ointment may be rubbed on the area of the bite. A previously prescribed antihistamine may be given orally.

Shock

Symptoms include irregular breathing and dilated pupils. Shock may occur with serious injury or fright to an animal. Keep the animal gently restrained, quiet, and warm. Elevate his head. Call your veterinarian.

Vomiting

Withhold food for twenty-four hours. Give ice cubes for two hours after vomiting stops. Then slowly increase the amount of water and foods given over a twenty-four hour period. Call your veterinarian.

Diarrhea

Withhold food for twelve to twenty-four hours. Give ice cubes only. Call your veterinarian.

Snake Bite (poisonous & nonpoisonous)

Symptoms include rapid swelling, skin puncture, pain, weakness, shock.

Stop all exercise to prevent spread of venom. Clean area. Many poisons damage the nerves or body tissue on contact. Call your veterinarian.

A TEASPOON OR TWO OF
ICE CREAM SEEMS TO
SETTLE A DOG'S STOMACH.

Seizures

Symptoms include salivation, loss of control of urine or stool, violent muscle twitching, loss of consciousness.

Move pet away from any objects that could be harmful. Use a blanket for padding and protection. Do not put yourself at risk by restricting the animal during the seizure. Time the seizure; it usually lasts only two to three minutes. Afterwards, keep the animal calm, quiet, and cool. Call your veterinarian.

Fractures

Symptoms include pain and an inability to use a leg.

Muzzle the animal and control any bleeding. Watch for any signs of shock. Do not try to reset a fracture. Transport the animal to the veterinarian immediately using a stretcher.

How to Create a Stretcher for Your Pet

A door, board, blanket or floor mat can be used as a stretcher to transport injured or weak animals.

How to Create a Muzzle for Your Pet

Use a strip of soft cloth, rope, necktie, or nylon stocking. Wrap around your pet's nose, under the chin, and tie behind the ears. Care must be taken when handling weak or injured animals. Even normally gentle pets can bite when in pain. Allow the animal to pant after handling by loosening or removing the muzzle. Do not use a muzzle in a case of vomiting. Small pets may be difficult to muzzle; a towel placed around a small pet's head will help control these animals.

I'll Get Right to the Point

A few years ago I was looking hard for an acupuncturist for dogs in the area where I live. I had a dog that could hardly walk because of arthritis. A local veterinarian told me of an acupuncturist just down the road who worked on dogs, and interestingly enough, he was also a vet. I took my dog there and found that not only did the treatment help his arthritis, but he seemed to become a puppy again. He was able to run, jump, and play the same way he did as a

puppy. Acupuncture is an interesting and different treatment. I would advise you to check this out if your dog suffers from arthritis.

Be careful that you watch the weight of your dog. An overweight dog will suffer more if he has arthritis. Exercise is important for a dog with this condition, as it is, of course, for all dogs. I have arthritis too and find that exercise is a great help. My friends with arthritis tell me they just want to stay home and rest when the pain acts up, but I find that when I walk just as hard as I can, the pain and discomfort are reduced. As near as I can tell, that holds true for my dogs too. Be sure that your dog is not out in the cold, however, since his arthritic condition will be aggravated by the cold, wet weather.

If your dog needs exercise and you are just not able to accompany him, think about hiring a youngster around eleven-years-old or older to come over to your house and take Fido for a walk. Many children would love to earn extra money to save toward buying that Bentley they've always wanted, and Fido will love the added attention a youngster can give. Remember, a bored dog will get into trouble. Think

about Fido's welfare and the health of your furniture and garden. Give Fido sufficient exercise and toys to minimize his boredom while you are away.

Take Your Dog Swimming, or There Are Two Pools of Thought

Swimming is wonderful for dogs, especially if they are arthritic. Swimming pools will work as well as lakes. But I have real trouble getting my Neapolitan mastiff into my bathtub. I'm afraid there are limitations.

Rehabilitation Swimming Pools

I built the first rehabilitation pool for Pandy, a Great Pyrenees. She was stolen from my house and jumped out of a truck on the highway and broke her spine. The vet recommended that we "put her down" because there was "no way she could make it." I was told she had a less than 5 percent chance of ever walking again. They operated and found that her spine was like toothpaste. Again the vet wanted to quit, but I said "no way." After the operation, Pandy could only use her front legs. I lifted her

hind legs with a large towel so she could go outside to go potty and for enjoying the fresh air. Remembering my own accident and to prevent bed sores, I got her a water bed. Then I thought that if I could get her into a pool, that might help her. I then built a pool in my backyard about eighteen by forty feet. When Pandy got into that water, her legs started to move, a little at a time. Before we knew it, she was walking again. Veterinarians from all over Colorado couldn't believe it. They started to send their dog patients over to my place for therapy. Soon, humans couldn't use the pool at all; it was reserved only for needy dogs. You should have seen the doggie hair in my filtration system! But the theraputic effects could not be denied. When I sold my house, I found it was extremely difficult to take my pool with me. So I got together with the Max Fund people in Denver, Colorado, an animal adoption agency, and built another therapeutic pool for animals. The facility treats injured animals with no known owners. It's manned by volunteers and paid for by meager donations from kind people. Vets from all over Colorado refer the owners of injured animals to

this shelter and pool where a therapist is on duty. It may be the only one like it in a shelter.

Incidentally, never let your dog ride in the back of a pickup truck. Many dogs are killed each year trying to jump out, or if they are tethered, jumping out and hanging themselves. There seems to be no laws against this practice, so each owner must be sensitive to the many dangers of allowing dogs to travel that way.

I Can't Afford Psychoanalysis for Spot

Did you know that dogs get depressed. It's not only humans. Dogs get depressed if they lose the friend who's been living with them for a long time or if they lose another dog that's been in the home for a while or for many other reasons. Many dogs have just died of a broken heart.

Here are some things that can help: Give your dog lots of extra attention. Turn on your radio when you're not there. Turn to a talk show. That helps keep Fido from getting bored. Or you can turn on the television. The sounds will be company for your dog. And again, I must repeat that exercise for your dog is not

only great for his physical well-being, but will help ensure that Fido won't be on Sigmund Freud's couch telling him the saga of a desperate puppyhood.

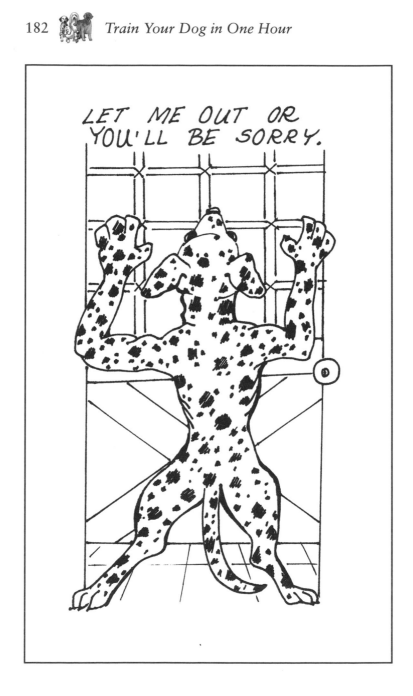

5

QUESTIONS AND ANSWERS

Dog owners often ask me questions. Some get asked more than others. So we are including some that may offer help to you as well.

Q. Sandy, please help! I leave my dog in the laundry room during the day while I'm at work. When I get home, my dog goes wild. After I let him out, for the longest time, he jumps and runs through the house and will not calm down. Is there anything I can do to control him?

A. How would you feel if you were locked up in the laundry room all day? What you need to do is install a doggy door. Any animal will go wild if kept in a confined place. You can place a portable kennel at the entrance of the dog door coming into the house. That way the dog will be able to enter, not have the run of the whole house, but can get out of the cold or bad weather. Make sure to leave food and lots of water.

Q. We have a Great Dane that weighs more than my husband. The dog loves to jump on everyone. We've had our dog for more than five years, and he's great in every way except for the jumping. Is there anything we can do to stop the bad behavior before he hurts someone?

A. This is an easy problem to correct. In a very firm voice, say "Spot, Down; "Spot, Down!" And at the same time raise your arm over your head. Bring your arm down and point to the ground. Always say the dog's name first, followed by a one word command. The Barker Stopper also works well for breaking your dog of this bad habit.

Q. What is the optimum age to train a dog?

A. The optimum age for a dog to be trained is anywhere from 12 weeks to 12 years. What I'm saying is that a dog is never too young or too old to be trained. The dog's name is the key to training. A dog that doesn't know his name cannot be trained. If you're giving your dog a brand new name because you just got him from the shelter, you must work with his name for at least one or two days before you can begin his training.

Q. We desperately need help on potty training our dog, Sadie. She just does NOT get the idea that she can't go in the house. We've tried everything. I think our biggest problem is that she is left alone all day.

A. Whatever you do, don't put Sadie's nose in the mess. Place your hand next to the soiled area. Hit your hand, just enough to make a noise, and say "Sadie, No! Sadie, No!" Clean up the soiled area with a paper towel. Take a little outside where you want Sadie to relieve herself, place it on the ground, and pointing to the area, strongly say "Sadie, Good! Sadie, Good!" The first time you see her go potty outside by herself make a big deal out of it followed by a small piece of her favorite treat. You will find that installing a dog door so she has access to the outside while you are away will be very helpful as well.

Q. We adopted a dog from the Humane Society recently. We were told she was neglected and abused. She is a loving dog but is skittish around my husband. She will let him pet her when he is sitting in his chair. She also comes to the bedroom to be petted every morning.

A. Your dog may have been mistreated by a man. It may take awhile for her to trust your husband, but from your description of her behavior, she is already warming to him. Have your husband buy the dog some special toys to play with. Then she can enjoy her playtime with him especially. But be patient and do not push her too fast.

Q. I have a year-old spayed dog. When she urinates on the grass, she leaves it yellow and burned. Any ideas?

A. All those brown spots in your yard are from over-fertilization of the grass by the ammonia in your dog's urine. Anything that reduces the ammonia content of the urine will minimize the burning. Try watering the burned area to wash away the ammonia. If that doesn't work, you might try acidifying your dog's urine by offering cranberry or clam juice to your dog. Not many dogs like the juices, so if that fails, you may wish to use d-methionine to acidify the urine. It should not be used for dogs with either kidney or liver problems, and you should always check with your veterinarian first. You can also put a wet finger in some baking soda and put it in your dog's drinking water. This technique often stops the problem.

Q. Our dog, Gizmo, a female Shih-Tzu, is one-and-a-half years old. She started urinating in the back room instead of going outside after being housebroken for more than a year. This started a couple of days after our baby was born.

A. This is a common problem. Gizmo feels that she has been replaced. Show her otherwise. Look at Gizmo and wrap your arms around her and say, "Gizmo, Mine; Gizmo, Mine," and then "Baby, Gizmo's; Baby, Gizmo's," Gizmo, Baby's; Gizmo, Baby's." This may sound silly but it works. You need to repeat this a couple of times a day so your dog understands that the baby is his also.

Be sure that you don't keep your dog away from the baby. Gizmo should then accept the new baby as a normal part of the household. Make a big deal out of it. Then, go to your baby and say or do the same thing showing how much you love your baby. Repeat this for a time over a period of several days or weeks. That should take care of the problem. It's also a good idea to bring a doll home before the baby comes. Put some baby clothes on it and pretend it's a real baby in front of your dog—a good rehearsal for the real appearance of baby.

Buy some toys for your dog before people come to see the new baby. Give your guests a dog toy to give to your dog before they go over to your baby. The dog thinks your guest has come to see him as well as your baby.

As for housebreaking, take Gizmo to your vet and make sure she doesn't have a medical problem. If she's fine, put your hand next to the spot where she has urinated, hit you hand and tell her, "Gizmo, No! Gizmo, No!" in a stern voice. Mop it up with a paper towel and have her follow you outside. Put the towel where you want her to go and say, "Gizmo, Good! Gizmo, Good!" Make a big deal every time you see her go outside. Give her a treat to let her know how happy you are with her good behavior.

Q. My five-year-old son is terrified of dogs. What can I do?

A. You've seen dogs chase cars with children sitting in them. That frightens a child. Children have been greeted by fifty pound dogs jumping and barking when they arrive at a home for a visit. We have been where big dogs run unmanaged through a house with no admonitions. Many dogs are badly behaved. Never tell a child there's nothing to be afraid of. There may be. To get rid of the fear, find a friend or acquaintance who has a well-trained dog and take your child to visit. With lots of good exposure, your child will probably get over his fear. Take it nice and easy.

Q. I have two wonderful dogs. The only problem I have with them is I just can't find a dog food they will eat. I try to change their food quite often so they don't get bored with the same thing, but I can't seem to make them happy. Have you ever heard of this before?

A. This is quite common with dogs who are given many different kinds of dog food. Give them one kind—perhaps recommended by your veterinarian—and don't change it. Most dogs don't like changing from one food to another. It just makes them very finicky eaters.

Q. My toy poodle drives us crazy when we are eating. She never stops begging, no matter what we do. She is never given any table food while we're eating, though we do give her some after we've finished. What do you recommend?

A. This is easy to cure. Don't give her ANY table scraps for at least a couple of hours after eating, or just put the scraps away in the refrigerator and make her wait until the next day. This way she won't associate her favorite scraps with your mealtime. NEVER feed her while you're eating. Extend your arm straight out, point your finger, and tell her, "Fido, Go! Fido, Go!" Make her leave the area while you're eating.

Q. How do you feel about wolf hybrids as a pet? I had two large dogs until I lost one to old age a couple of months ago, and the other dog appears quite lonely. I'd like to get her another friend.

A. I would not recommend a wolf hybrid. If you were getting it as an only pet, that's another story. Wolf hybrids can live with another dog for years, love each other, then one day get into a fight and the wolf will kill your other dog. This is very common. Remember, the wolf hybrid is still partly wild.

Q. My eleven-month-old Golden Retriever wants to eat my furniture. I have sprinkled every product you can find that's supposed to stop this and nothing has worked. Do you know of a magic product I haven't found yet?

A. Yes, but it's not a product. Just put your hand on the object he is biting, palm up, and slap your hand, looking directly at your pet and saying, "Fido, No; Fido, No!" with a strong authoritative voice. Turn around and put a toy in his mouth and say "Fido, Good; Fido, Good." Wait twenty minutes and go back and tell him how happy you are that he hasn't touched the furniture and say, "Fido, Good; Fido, Good." Do this three or four times when you get ready to leave home. When your dog leaves the furniture alone, get excited and praise your dog. Also give him a treat. Turn this into a positive communication.

Q. I'm getting ready to fly to California, and I'm taking my dog. Is there anything I need to know?

A. Ask the airline if the luggage compartment is pressurized and heated. Many aren't. If your pet is small enough to put in an airline carrier that will fit under your seat, do that. Your pet could become frightened and require some tender loving care. You also need to get a health certificate from your vet before flying.

You may want to give your dog a sedative. It's very hard on many dogs to fly without one. Talk to your vet and find out what he suggests.

Q. I'm thinking of getting a dog, but I don't know what kind to get. Ideas?

A. Dogs of all breeds are loving and desirable if treated and trained properly. Do you live in an apartment? Are you an excitable person? Would shedding dogs bother you? Do you have small children? Do you have a large or small yard? Look at yourself, your lifestyle, and everyone who will share the responsibility for the animal, then investigate different breeds.

Q. Do you have any advice on separation anxiety? Our dog follows us from room to room when she knows that we're going out.

A. Separation anxiety is common. Following you from room to room is typical. Try leaving a radio on and make sure she has lots of toys to play with while you're gone. You might try leaving for short periods so that your dog will know you are coming back. A change of routines can also help; if you always put your coat on last, try putting it on before you start walking out the door. If you usually pick up your keys last, put them in your pocket first. These changes often help to calm your dog.

Q. I have a two-year-old Rottweiler I adopted last July. She is a good dog, but she licks all the time, not only me but everything and everyone. I tell her "no" but that doesn't work. What can I do?

A. The word "no" is not enough. You need to say her name and then the one word command. That will get her attention. With the furniture, blankets, etc., put your hand on the object, palm up, and hit your hand—not hard, but with a clapping sound, and say her name and "No!" Always be sure that your dog is not suffering a particular disease that causes the continuous licking. Another individual wrote to us telling us about their eight-year-old Dachshund who died from a form of anemia. The owner's first reaction to the licking was that it was a behavioral problem. After two weeks of trying to break her of this, she was taken to our vet, and the owner learned the awful truth. It was too late. So always be aware and consider whether a trip to the vet may be the best thing to do to be certain.

Q. I've been thinking of giving a puppy as a gift to my girlfriend for her birthday. Do you think that giving animals as a gift is a good idea?

A. No, it isn't. There are tales upon tales of unasked for animals given with good intentions, pets that end up in the nearest animal shelter because the person receiving the gift is unprepared to handle all that goes with owning a new puppy. People who want dogs should make these decisions on their own. Resist the temptation to give a pet as a gift. What was meant as a loving gift can turn into a nightmare for the gift recipient and the dog. When the fun of having a new "toy" wears off, the reality of the care of the animal sets in, and the new owner often gives up and gets rid of the dog. As an alternative, you can go to a pet shelter and get a gift certificate. If the person doesn't want a dog, he can use the certificate as a tax deduction. Animal shelters need all the donations they can get.

Q. Is it a good idea to get a dog from an animal shelter?

A. The local shelter is a great place to pick out a new animal. Every size, shape, and breed is often available, and you can find purebred animals, delightful mixed breeds, some trained, others untrained, all waiting for someone to love them. And you are offering the animal a new chance for life. What a great treat for all concerned.

Q. We have a ten-year-old dog with a strange habit. We got him from a shelter when he was three years old. When we leave the house, he finds my or my husband's slippers or clothing and hides them in corners or behind furniture. He only does this when we are gone from the house. What does all this mean?

A. Your dog is bored when you are gone and is also expressing separation anxiety. The first thing you need to do is get him his own toys and put them in his own toy box. The next time you find articles of clothing hidden, pick them up, put your hand on top of them, palm up, then hit your hand, looking at your dog saying "Fido, No; Fido, No." Then pick up a toy and put it in his mouth and say, "Fido, Good; Fido, Good." Repeat this two or three times. He'll get the idea. It also helps if slippers and clothes are put away out of reach of your dog.

Q. I have a dog that has bad breath. Is this natural?

A. Generally, dogs don't have bad breath. The most likely cause is a dental problem. It may also indicate other problems, such as a digestive disorder or other disease. You will want to include a full dental checkup as part of your next visit to your vet. There are different kinds of toothpaste for dogs, but you don't want to give them a lot of it. It's also helpful to put a bit of charcoal in your dog's food, but check with your vet to be sure you are using the correct amount relative to the size of your dog. Excellent foods for helping to keep your dog's teeth clean are almost any kind of fruits and vegetables, especially raw carrots. Dry food works better than wet, and, believe it or not, there are dog sprays to help make Fido's breath as pleasant as a newborn babe.

Q. Could you tell me why my dog digs holes in the yard? I have a big yard and I don't like to chain him up. But I'm considering it. My dog is part Chow, part Shar-Pei. She also digs out the sprinkler heads. I'm at a loss as to what to do.

A. Dogs love to dig for all kinds of reasons and can certainly mess up a yard. I suggest a device called a Barker Stopper or Super Barker Stopper. It's designed to stop your dog from barking, but it is also effective in stopping digging. When you see her digging, push a button on the unit that gives off a high-pitched sound. Say her name first, and a sharp "No!" This will stop her. I hate to see any dog chained.

Q. I have a nine-year-old unneutered part Collie whom I love. The only problem is he jumps all over me and is really hyper. What should I do?

A. You should get your dog neutered. It will make him calmer, and it is much better for health reasons. You also need to teach him basic obedience. Raise your arm and move it quickly down, pointing to the ground. At the same time, say your dog's name, then with a sharp command, say "Down!" You can also use the Barker Stopper for this behavior. Then reward him with a tiny treat.

Q. I have a dog who is afraid of thunder and lightning. He panics and digs at things looking for a safe place. How can I calm his fears?

A. Go to your local music store and buy a cassette or disk of thunder and lightning, or tape a storm yourself the next time a storm occurs. Begin by playing the tape very softly at first, playing with your dog and acting like everything is just wonderful. Turn the tape up each time you play it over the next couple of days, continuing to play with the dog as if there is nothing unusual happening. He will get used to the noise and, because you are calm, you should find that when the next storm arrives, he should feel much more comfortable. Do not hold the dog and pamper him during the storm. You're just telling him that something is wrong, and it defeats your purpose.

A Final Thought

There is magic in having a dog, a bond between animal and human that reaches deep into our heart. Positive dog training with love, consistency, and care is the key to a happy relationship for you and your pet. Your dog will give you unquestioning, complete, and rewarding love in return.

BIBLIOGRAPHY

American Kennel Club. *The Complete Dog Book*. New York: Howell Book House, 1992.

Baer, Ted. *Communicating with Your Dog*. New York: Barron's Educational Series, Inc., 1989.

Benjamin, Carol Lea. *Second-Hand Dog*. New York: Howell Book House, Inc., 1988.

Capuzzo, Michael. *Wild Things: The Wacky and Wonderful Truth About the Animal Kingdom*. New York: Ballantine Books, 1995.

Caras, Roger. *Roger Caras' Treasury of Great Dog Stories*. New York: E. P. Dutton, 1988.

Caras, Roger. *The Roger Caras Dog Book*. New York: M. Evans & Co., 1992.

Caren, Stanley. *The Intelligence of Dogs*. New York: The Free Press, 1994.

Comfort, David. *The First Pet History of the World*. New York: Fireside/Simon & Schuster, 1994.

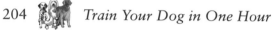
Denenberg, R. V., and Eric Seidman. *The Dog Catalog.* New York: Grosset & Dunlap, 1977.

Fogle, Bruce. *ASPCA Complete Dog Training Manual.* Sondon: Dorling Kindersley, 1994.

Holmes, John and Mary. *Looking After Your Dog.* New York: Arco Publishing, Inc., 1981.

Kelly, Niall. *Presidential Pets.* New York: Abbeville Press, 1992.

Kilcommons, Brian and Michael Capuzzo. *Mutts, America's Dogs.* New York: Warner Books, Inc., 1996.

Kilcommons, Brian, and Sarah Willson. Childproofing Your Dog. New York: Warner Books, 1994.

McLennan, Bardi. *Dogs and Kids.* New York: Maxwell Macmillan, 1993.

Pryor, Karen. *Don't Shoot the Dog.* New York: Bantam Books, 1985.

Tarrant, Bill. *The Magic of Dogs.* New York: Lyons & Burford, 1995.

Winckur, Jon, ed. *Mondo Canine: A Treasury of Quotations, Anecdotes, Essays and Lore in Celebration of Doggie Joie-de-Vivre.* New York: E. P. Dutton, 1991.

Yamazaki, Tetsu. *Legacy of the Dog: The Ultimate Illustrated Guide to Over 200 Breeds.* New York: Chronicle Books, 1995.

Index

—A—

Acupuncture for your dog, 171
Afghan Hound, 49, 51
Age of dog training, 185
Akita, 47, 51
Antifreeze, harm your dog, 39
Arthritis, 171, 173

—B—

Barker Stopper, 121, 184, 199, 200
Basset Hound, 49
Bathing your dog, 131
Beagle, 35, 49
Begging from the table, 111
Bernese, 47
Bichon Frise, 53
Bite wounds, 159
Bleeding, 161
Bloodhound, 49
Boston Terrier, 53
Boxer, 47, 53

Breathing, when your dog stops, 161
Breed differences, 47
Breeder, 33
Breeds of dogs, 51
Brushing your dog's teeth, 149
Bulldog, 53
Bullmastif, 53
Burns, 163

—C—

Cairn Terrier, 55
Chewing, 29, 37, 41, 79, 103, 113, 115, 117, 119, 121
Chewing on the furniture, 113
Chihuahua, 55
Children and dogs, 15, 17, 19, 21, 23, 31, 41, 55, 59, 61, 63, 65, 67, 73, 85, 89, 99, 107, 113, 173, 189, 194
Choke collar, 123
Chow Chow, 47, 55

Collie, 47, 53, 55, 199
Comfort for your dog, 71
Communication from your
  dog, 77
Consistency in training, 77

—D—

Dalmatian, 55
Depression and your dog, 179
Diarrhea, 135, 163, 167
Digging in the garden, 119
Doberman, 47, 57
Dog bites, 21
Dog door, 157
Dog shelter, 5
Doghouse, 45
Dogs and babies, 23
Dogs in the suburbs, 31
Dogs, get bored, 35
Dogs, more than one, 35, 107

—E—

Elkhound, 47
English Sheepdog, 57
Exercise and your dog, 145

—F—

Food and dogs, 135
Foreign Objects, 165
Fox Terrier, 57

—G—

German Shepherd, 57

Golden Retriever, 17, 59, 149,
  192
Great Dane, 59, 184
Great Pyrenees, 31, 47, 175
Greyhound, 17, 19, 49, 115,
  139, 155
Grooming your dog, 149

—H—

Happy Walker, 125
Heat stroke, 165
Hot weather and your pet,
  145
Husky, 47
Hypothermia, 43

—I—

Insect bites, 165
Instincts of your dog, 75
Irish Setter, 1, 17, 19, 59

—J—

Japanese Chin, 59

—K—

Keeshond, 59

—L—

Labrador Retriever, 17
Language and dogs, 75
Lhasa Apso, 61
Losing patience, 85

—M—

Maltese, 61
Mental stimulation for your
   dog, 69
Miniature Schnauzer, 61
Mixed breeds, 11, 27, 197
Muzzle, 171

—N—

Nails, cutting your dog's, 147
Neuter your dog, 41, 43, 199
New dog, prepare your home,
   37

—P—

Papillon, 61
Pekinese, 61
Pointer, 49
Pomeranian, 63
Poodle, 63
Positive reinforcement, 87
Positive stimulation for your
   dog, 69
Potty training, 39, 101
Preserving your space, 109
Pug, 63
Puppies, 15, 17, 29, 31, 33,
   39, 41, 43, 45, 71, 73, 93,
   95, 99, 103, 105, 113,
   133, 135, 141, 151, 153,
   171, 173, 181, 195, 196
Purebreds, 11

—R—

Retriever, 17, 33, 49, 59, 61,
   149, 192
Rewards, 69, 71, 89, 200
Rottweiler, 194

—S—

Saint Bernard, 63
Saluki, 63
Samoyed, 63
Schipperke, 65
Schnauzer, 65
Scottish Terrier, 65
Seizures, 169
Setter, 1, 17, 19, 49, 59
Sex characteristics of dogs, 49
Shelter, 5, 11, 13, 15, 17, 29,
   41, 75, 113, 147, 179,
   185, 196, 197
Shelter or a breeder, 33
Shepherd, 31, 47
Shock, 167
Siberian husky, 65
Snake bite, 167
Socializing experiences, 73,
   153
Spaniel, 27, 49, 55, 57
Spay your dog, 41, 187
Stretcher, creating one, 169
Super Barker Stopper, 121,
   199
Survival instincts, your dog,
   71
Swimming pools for your dog,
   175

—T—

Teaching your dog to come, 89
Teaching your dog to lie down, 97
Teaching your dog to sit, 95
Teaching your dog to stay, 99
Terrier, 49
Thinking, your dog, 69
Thunder and lightning, 125
Toothpaste for dogs, 198
Toys for your dog, 117
Treats, 39, 71, 79, 89, 93, 103, 111, 113, 127, 155, 157, 159, 163, 171, 173, 177, 186, 189, 193, 197, 200
Tying your dog, 39

—U—

Upset stomach, 139

—V—

Veterinarian, 33, 41, 81, 149, 161, 163, 165, 167, 169, 171, 187, 190
Vomiting, 167

—W—

Water, give dogs plenty, 141
Weimaraner, 65
Welsh Corgi, 67
What kind of dog for you, 31
Whippet, 49
Wolf hybrid, 192

—Y—

Yorkshire Terrier, 67